THE
LITTLE
BOOK OF
SCOTTISH
RAIN

THE LITTLE BOOK OF
SCOTTISH
RAIN

RON BUTLIN
ILLUSTRATED BY TIM KIRBY

BIRLINN

First published in 2018 by
Birlinn Limited
West Newington House
10 Newington Road
Edinburgh
EH9 1QS

Text copyright © Ron Butlin 2018
Line illustrations copyright © Tim Kirby 2018

ISBN 978 178027 557 4

British Library Cataloguing in Publication Data
A catalogue record for this book is available from the
British Library.

Designed by James Hutcheson
Typeset by Initial Typesetting Services, Edinburgh
Printed and bound by Bell & Bain Ltd, Glasgow

MULL WEATHER

It rained and rained and rained and rained,
The average was well maintained;
And when our fields were simply bogs,
It started raining cats and dogs.
After a drought of half an hour,
There came a most refreshing shower;
And then the queerest thing of all,
A gentle rain began to fall.
Next day 'twas pretty fairly dry,
Save for a deluge from the sky.
This wetted people to the skin,
But after that the rain set in.
We wondered what's the next we'd get,
As sure as fate we got more wet.
But soon we'll have a change again,
And we shall have
... a drop of rain.

ANON

INTRODUCTION

There is little point in coming to Scotland and complaining about the weather. When I was young and used to holiday on Mull, I came across the short poem "Mull Weather", which was undoubtedly written from the heart but which misses the endless variety of rain that Scotland enjoys.

As I started to write this introduction, the sun was beating down. It was also raining. The rain died back to a mere smirr. However, it has now resumed as a torrential flood. How it is doing this from a largely cloudless sky only the Almighty knows. Before the afternoon is out I will have experienced a whole range of other forms of precipitation to delight and torment.

My evening walk will either begin wet and end dry, or start dry and end wet. Or it may simply pour throughout.

But however the rain comes down, the end result is always the same, and without it the hills would not be so green, the trees would not grow, the rivers would not flow and the light would not have the iridescent quality we so associate with the Highlands.

This book is a celebration of the salient feature of Scotland's climatic system – and well might we celebrate, as the rain will still come down no matter what. The Eskimos may have more than fifty words for snow. Welcome to Scotland's unique contribution to the language of weather.

HUGH ANDREW
Summer 2018
Mull

A RECIPE FOR WHISKY –
A HANDFUL OF SCOTCH MIST
SQUEEZED INTO A GLASS.

SCOTCH MIST

A THICK, WET FOG THAT
MAKES THE MOUNTAINS,
GLENS AND EVERYONE IN
THEM DISAPPEAR

SHETLAND WIND AND RAIN
CAN LIFT YOU OFF YOUR FEET,
TO SEND YOU FLYING THROUGH THE AIR
OR SWIMMING DOWN THE STREET.

UPLOWSIN
(SHETLAND)

VIOLENT RAINS, OFTEN FOLLOWING A THAW

RAIN STOTTED OFF ADAM, RAIN STOTTED OFF MOSES,
ATHENIAN BEARDS AND ROMAN NOSES;
IT STOTS OFF NESSIE WHEN SHE COMES UP FOR AIR,
THIS STOTTING RAIN STOTS EVERYWHERE!

STOTS
(SCOTS)

TO BOUNCE, AS WHEN RAIN
BOUNCES OFF PAVEMENTS,
PEOPLE'S HEADS, ETC.

'IT'S DREICH OOT THERE.'
THERE'S A NOD OF THE HEAD
FROM THE MAN WHO'D RATHER STAY IN HIS BED.

DREICH
(SCOTS)

WHEN THE WEATHER LOOKS
SERIOUSLY DEPRESSED,
WITH DISMAL, SCOWLING
CLOUDS THAT ALMOST
TOUCH THE ROOFS
OF PEOPLE'S HOUSES

DREEP AND DREEP AND DREEP AND DREEP,
THE RAIN'S SLOWED DOWN AND FALLEN ASLEEP.
DREEP AND DREEP AND DREEP SOME MORE,
THE WIND YAWNS AND STARTS TO SNORE.

DREEP
(SCOTS, FROM 'DRIP')

A SLOW, STEADY DOWNPOUR

IF YOU'VE HOLES IN YOUR ROOF
AND THE WEATHER TURNS PLOWTERY,
IT HARDLY MATTERS IF YOU'RE INSIDE OR OUT-ERY!

PLOWTERY

RAIN THAT FALLS IN A
KIND OF LAZY,
HALF-HEARTED SHOWER

A GANDIEGOW SUITS SCOTS LIKE ME
OUR CLOTHES GET WASHED,
OUR GERMS GET SQUASHED,
AND WE GET SHOWERED FOR FREE!

GANDIEGOW
(SCOTS)

A HEAVY RAIN, A REAL GIFT
TO THE THRIFTIER SCOT

IF YOU'RE DROOKIT, YOU'RE DRENCHED,
A WRINGING WET HEAP
THAT'S WETTER THAN DIVERS DOWN IN THE DEEP!

DROOKIT
(SCOTS)

TO BE TOTALLY
TOP-TO-TOE
SOAKED THROUGH

RAIN THAT CASCADES
COMES DOWN IN FLUDDERS,
FROM CELESTIAL COWS
WITH GALACTIC-SIZED UDDERS!

IN FLUDDERS
(SCOTS, FROM 'FLOODS')

A TRULY MASSIVE DOWNPOUR

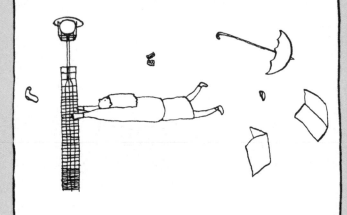

A RIGHT BAFFIN WE'RE GETTING
OUT IN THE STREET,
WE'RE WHIRLED AND BIRLED
RIGHT OFF OUR FEET.
SPLAT IN THE GUTTER! SPLAT UP THE WALL!
SPLAT, SPLAT, GETTING NOWHERE AT ALL!

BAFFIN
(SCOTS)

THE BEATING FORCE OF
WIND AND RAIN

LOOKS LIKE IT'S
JUST PASSING
THROUGH

BLEETERS COME AND BLEETERS GO,
THEY NEVER, EVER STAY -
IF IT ISN'T RAINING NOW
MORE RAIN IS ON THE WAY.

BLEETERS
(CAITHNESS)

RAIN THAT COMES IN ABRUPT GUSTS

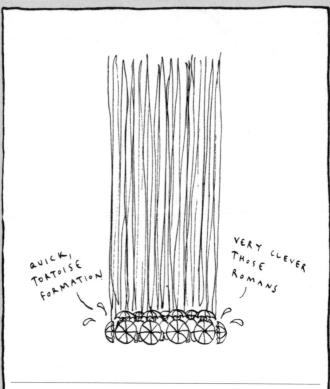

UARS COME DOWN UPON US ALL,
GAEL AND LALLANDER, SMALL AND TALL.
THERE WERE UARS BEFORE A HUMAN WAS BORN,
THERE'LL BE UARS LONG AFTER HUMANS ARE GONE.

UAR
(GAELIC)

A WATERSPOUT OF HEAVY, HEAVY RAIN

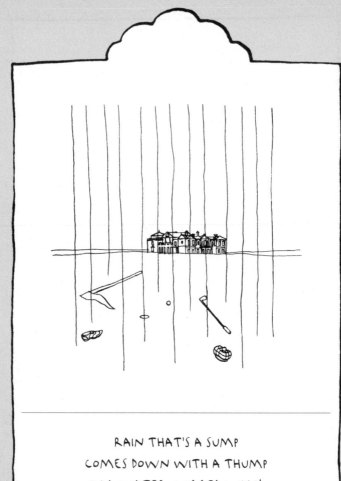

RAIN THAT'S A SUMP
COMES DOWN WITH A THUMP
IN A WATER-LOGGED LUMP!

SUMP
(FIFE)

A SUDDEN TOTAL DELUGE

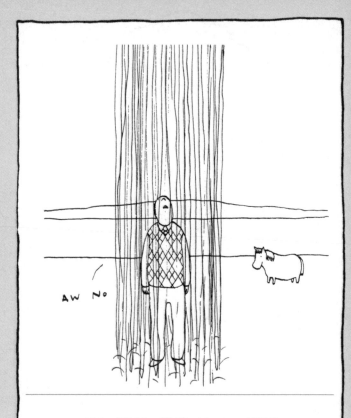

UMPLIST RAIN'S FROM NOWHERE,
IT FALLS FROM AN EMPTY SKY.
I WISH IT WOULD GO BACK THERE,
BUT IT DOESN'T EVEN TRY!

UMPLIST
(SHETLAND)

A DOWNPOUR OUT OF THE BLUE

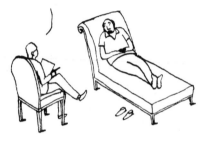

HAVE YOU TRIED
STANDING OUT IN
THE RAIN?

LET SMIRR THERAPY MAKE YOU WHOLE,
LET ITS SLOWED-DOWN SYLLABLE
SOOTHE YOUR SOUL.
BE IN THE SMIRR!
CHANT EACH LETTER,
FEEL BETTER AND BETTER
AS YOU GET WETTER AND WETTER.

SMIRR
(SCOTS)

FINE DRIZZLE

I THINK THERE'S A
NEOLITHIC CHAMBERED
CAIRN HERE SOMEWHERE

AAARGH

WHEN THERE'S A ROOST IN ORKNEY
NOTHING'S WHAT IT SEEMS –
LIFE GETS MISTED OVER
LOST IN DROWSY DREAMS.

ROOST
(ORKNEY)

A PARTICULARLY
THICK MIST

AARGH

WHEN THE WEATHER GETS BLASHY,
THE SLEET AND RAIN
ARE BLOWN IN YOUR FACE AGAIN AND AGAIN.
WHEN YOU TURN TO GO HOME,
THE WIND WILL TURN TOO –
FOR BLASHY CHILL WEATHER JUST LOVES
BLASHING YOU!

BLASHY
(SCOTS)

RAIN AT ITS WETTEST AND MOST BLOWN-ABOUT

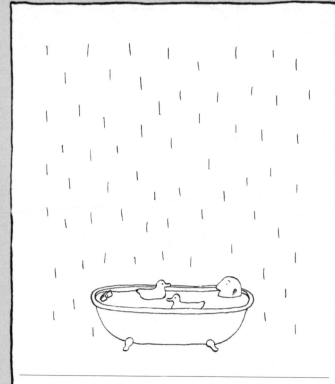

SCOTTISH DUCKS ARE LUCKY DUCKS,
MORE PUDDLES THAN THEY CAN PADDLE IN,
THE WATER'S WETTER, THE MUD TASTES BETTER
TO McMURDO AND McMADELINE!

'GOOD FOR THE DUCKS'

A GREETING THAT IMPLIES
THIS DREARY WET WEATHER
MUST BE GOOD FOR
SOMETHING

RAFF! RAFF! RAFF!
THE RAIN CUTS ME IN HALF,
THE WIND GETS IN AND BLOWS AROUND,
A HOWLING, GROWLING TRUMPET SOUND
THAT MAKES ME WANT TO LAUGH!
RAFF! RAFF! RAFF!

RAFF
(SCOTS)

A SHARP SHOWER

THIS SOUNDLESS RAIN DESCENDS UNSEEN
UNTIL YOU'RE SOAKED RIGHT THROUGH.
AN ORCADIAN HAGGAR'S NOT JUST WET,
BUT WETTER THAN THE WETTEST WET CAN GET.
POOR ... SODDEN ... YOU.

HAGGAR
(ORKNEY)

WHEN RAIN DRIFTS DOWN AS
A GENTLE AND VERY WET
CARESS

THE DRIV THAT'S HURRYING OVER THE SEA
IS COMING FOR YOU AND COMING FOR ME.
NO HAT? NO BROLLY?
WE'LL GET WHAT WE'RE DUE -
TO BE SOAKED TO THE SKIN, BOTH ME AND YOU!

DRIV
(ORKNEY AND SHETLAND)

ONE OF MANY, MANY WORDS
NEEDED TO DESCRIBE THE
VAST QUANTITIES OF RAIN
THAT FALL ON THESE
ISLANDS

SOME RAIN TRIES TO WIGGLE
AND SOME RAIN TO WAGGLE,
EVEN PRANCE AND DANCE,
BUT THE BEST RAIN WILL DAGGLE.
TO THE SURGE OF THE WIND,
IT WILL SWIRL AND SWAY,
HOW IT LOVES TO SHIMMY AND DAGGLE ALL DAY!

DAGGLE

TO RAIN IN TORRENTS

AYE, STILL
RAINING
WILLIAM

SMUGGY RAIN'S GREAT IF YOU'RE IN THE MOOD
FOR A GENTLE DRENCHING THAT SOAKS YOU GOOD.

AND IT'S NO USE COMPLAINING, NO USE AT ALL
FOR WINDS MUST BLOW AND RAINS MUST FALL.

SMUGGY
(ABERDEEN)

THE FINE QUALITY OF DRIZZLE

I'M THINKING OF NOTHING, TAKING MY EASE
WHEN A PLYPE OF RAIN HITS ME.
PLYPE ON MY HEAD, ON MY NOSE AND MY KNEES!
I'M SOAKED, IF YOU PLEASE!

PLYPE

A SUDDEN DASH OF RAIN

THANKS TO THAT DAG OUR WOODPILE IS SODDEN.
OUR FIRE'S GOING OUT,
COME NIGHT WE'LL BE FROZEN.
SOME POTS AND PANS TO CATCH THE LEAKS.
AN AXE TO THAT WARDROBE.
IT'LL LAST US FOR WEEKS!

DAG

A HEAVY, NEVER-ENDING DRIZZLE

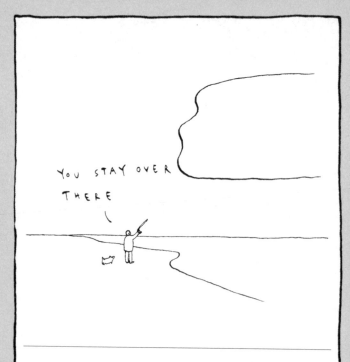

THE BREATH OF A GOD WHO'S FAR OUT AT SEA
(HE DESPISES US ALL, I.E. YOU AND ME)
IS SHROUDING OUR LAND IN SUNLESS GREY LAYERS.

LET HIM SQUAT ON COLD WATERS!
LET HIM WAIT FOR OUR PRAYERS!

HAAR

SEA-MIST, ESPECIALLY ON THE EAST COAST

THE SKY'S GONE BLACK, THE WIND IS A ROAR,
A BOWDER'S BATTERING AT OUR DOOR.
IT HAMMERS THE ROOF.
THERE'S NOWHERE TO HIDE.
WHEN A BOWDER'S ABOUT YOU BEST STAY INSIDE!

BOWDER

A HEAVY RAIN STORM

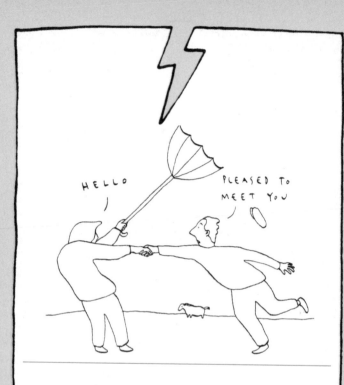

AFTER GUSTING THEIR WORST
AND DRENCHING THEIR BEST,
MESSRS. WIND AND RAIN HAVE STOPPED FOR A REST.
THEN SOON AS THEY CAN,
THEY'RE BACK ON THEIR FEET,
GUSTING AND DRENCHING THE PEOPLE THEY MEET.

AFLAK
(ORKNEY AND SHETLAND)

THE OCCASIONAL PAUSE
IN A STORM

DOWN THE GLEN AND OVER THE BRAE
A PERIGEAN BLAST IS COMING OUR WAY,
LET'S SHUT FAST THE WINDOWS,
BOLT TIGHT THE DOOR,
LET'S DRINK TO THE STORM,
THEN POUR OUT SOME MORE!

PERIGEAN BLAST

COASTAL WIND AND RAIN ASSOCIATED WITH STRONG TIDES

I HATE WHEN WEATHER'S HUTHER
AND CAN'T MAKE UP ITS MIND.
IF IT'S SUNNY FOR A MOMENT,
THE RAIN'S NOT FAR BEHIND.

HUTHER
(SCOTS)

INTERMITTENT RAIN

THE FIRST-EVER GOSELET WAS HIGH IN THE SKY,
SCOTLAND WAS DESERT AND LOOKING TOO DRY
TILL THE FIRST-EVER RAINDROP DROPPED.

SINCE THEN, THAT GOSELET'S HARDLY STOPPED!

GOSELET
(ABERDEEN)

A DRENCHING DOWNPOUR

HERE'S THE RAIN WE LOVE THE BEST,
A BETTER RAIN THAN ALL THE REST.
IT SOOTHES OUR TROUBLES, CURES OUR ILLS -
BETTER MEDICINE THAN TAKING PILLS!

UISGE
(GAELIC)

WATER AS IN *UISGE BEATHA*,
THE WATER OF LIFE,
I.E. WHISKY

THESE RUNES IN THE SKY ARE READ AS ROGS,
THEIR MESSAGE IS ALWAYS CLEAR —
SOON IT'LL BE RAINING CATS AND DOGS,
AND YOU'D BETTER DISAPPEAR!

ROGS
(SHETLAND)

LINES OF CLOUDS
PORTENDING RAIN

A SCOW'S A BOAT THAT'LL KEEP YOU AFLOAT
WHETHER YOU'RE SOBER OR DRUNK.
IN SCOTS A SCOW'S THE STORMIEST WEATHER
AND YOUR BOAT'S ALREADY SUNK!

SCOW
(SCOTS)

A WIND AND RAIN STORM

SCOTTISH FOLK DON'T MAKE A FUSS
WHEN WIND AND RAIN BLAST IN A RUS.
BLOWN ABOUT, WASHED DOWN THE STREET?
WE'LL DANCE ROUND THE SKY ON HAPPY WET FEET!

RUS
(SCOTS)

STORMY, HEAVY RAIN

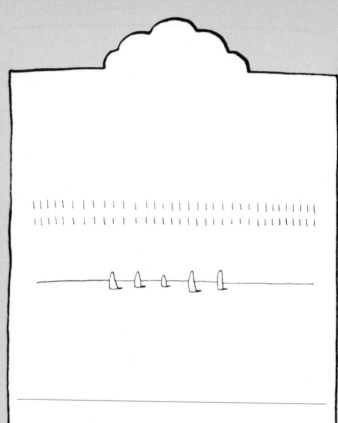

A FISS OF RAIN'S SO STEADY, SO STILL,
KEEPS FALLING BUT NEVER COMES DOWN.
TIME GOES SLOW, THE MINUTES STOP
AND THE NEXT HOUR NEVER COMES ROUND.

FISS
(ORKNEY)

DRIZZLE

CHEERFUL RAIN COMES DINGING DOWN
INVITING US TO DANCE.
LET'S PRAY THE SPRAY WILL DING ALL DAY,
LET'S WALTZ WHILE WE'VE THE CHANCE!

DINGIN DOUN
(SCOTS)

WHEN RAINDROPS ARE
FALLING SO HARD THEY
ALMOST BOUNCE

SMIZZLE'S A DRIZZLE THAT STARTS AS A SMIRR
LIKE A WINKLE STARTS AS A WINK.
SO WATCH WHAT YOU SAY,
FOR ALL WORDS BETRAY
A GREAT DEAL MORE THAN YOU THINK!

SMIZZLE
(SCOTS)

A LIGHT, VERY RELAXED RAIN

TO BE HATLESS IN THE DRIVING RAIN,
IS REALLY MOST REFRESHING –
THE FREEZING WATER COOLS THE BRAIN,
EACH ICE-COLD DROP'S A BLESSING!

KAAVIE
(SCOTS)

DRIVING RAIN, FROM NORSE *KAV*, SNOWFALL

WHEN THE RAIN'S AN ICY SCUDDER
WE'RE MADE TO TREMBLE AND SHUDDER,
LIKE SHIPS OUT AT SEA, AS LOST AS CAN BE,
WITHOUT MASTS, SAILS OR RUDDER.

SCUDDER
(SCOTS)

COLD DRIVING SHOWERS

A MILLION, MILLION RAINDROPS LACED TOGETHER
SCREEN THE WORLD FROM VIEW.
CLEARWATER TAPESTRY, A SODDEN SHROUD,
A SMUE.

SMUE
(SCOTS)

TO DRIZZLE DENSELY;
A DENSE DRIZZLE

BAD ANGELS ROAM THE SKY
SPITTING DOWN ON FOLK WHO ARE DRY.
WE SHOULD BE GRATEFUL. HOW WE WOULD CURSE
IF THEY GAVE UP SPITTING –
FOR SOMETHING MUCH WORSE!

SPITTER
(SCOTS)

SMALL DRIVING PARTICLES
OF RAIN OR SNOW

WHEN RAIN FROM THE EAST
MEETS RAIN FROM THE WEST
I'M SOAKED RITH THROUGH TO MY YS AND MY VEST.
SO I KEEP OUT OF PUDDLES AND STARE AT THE SKY,
HOPING THE WIND WILL BLOW ME DRY.

YILLEN
(SHETLAND)

A SHOWER WITH WIND

WHO NEEDS A DIAMOND'S WELL-CUT SPARKLE?
WHO NEEDS THE SAPPHIRE'S PRICEY GLINT?
A WATERGOW AFFIRMS OUR LIVES
EVEN WHEN WE'RE SKINT!

A WATERGOW'S A PROMISE
GOOD WEATHER'S ON ITS WAY –
BUT RAIN GIVES LIFE SO LET'S GIVE THANKS
SCOTTISH RAIN IS HERE TO STAY!

WATERGOW
(SCOTS)

A RAINBOW